Stop Dog Aggression

Everything You Need to Know to Handle Dog Behavioral Problems

By Daniel Joseph

Copyright © Daniel Joseph

All rights reserved. No part of this book may be reproduced, copied, stored, or transmitted in any form or by any means, electronic, photographic, or mechanical, including photocopying, recording, or in any information storage and retrieval systems, without prior written permission of the author or publisher, except where permitted by law.

Also by Daniel Joseph

Puppy Training Book: The Quick Guide for New Owners

Contents

Introduction 5

Different Types of Dogs 7

Finding the Right Breeder 13

Is Your Dog a Commonly Known Aggressive Breed? 17

Normal Problems That Dogs Have Concerning Aggression 23

Signs to Recognize 25

The Reasoning Behind Your Dog's Aggression 29

Ways to Stop Aggression in Your Dog 33

How to Control Redundant Barking 41

Stopping Dog Aggression over Food 45

The Dog's Biting Problems - What You Can Do 47

What to Do If Your Dog Displays Early Warning Signs 53

Things You Should and Shouldn't Do Concerning Dog Aggression 59

Common Dog Aggression Training Guidelines 63

Dog Fighting, What To Do About It 65

Conclusion 67

Introduction

You might say that training dogs is difficult, which is true, but it can be very easy if you have the right information, knowledge and way to go about training them.

It is vital that you take your time getting your dogs, or dog trained so they can behave properly in your home, or anywhere else.

There are many things that go into how successful your dog's training can be.

Different Types of Dogs

There are a lot of types and breeds of dogs, over a hundred.

Knowing how those types of dogs act and behave has to do with its breed. Such as there are dogs that are purebred, and there are mixes.

Purebreds are dogs that have only been bred with their breed, and have a pure ancestry or lineage.

Mixes are dogs that have another breed or several breeds in their lineage, and have mixed traits.

Assuming you are thinking about buying a new dog or puppy, you should first figure out what breed or type of dog you want.

Here are some common and popular breeds of dogs.

German Shepherds

These types of canines originally use to help farmers in herding.

They are brilliantly smart and trainable. They have a large and sturdy build, and because of that they are often used as police or military working dogs.

A lot of them are also used as guides for the blind. German shepherds are massive and strong canines with a variety of possible fur colors. The most common colors are gray, cream, black, or white.

Labradors

Labradors are quick and outgoing canines that have a wide range of attributes. A lot of them are also called retrievers and are used as guide canines for the blind, similar to German Shepherds.

Labradors enjoy playing with their owners, and chewing on various objects. Labradors are also very sensitive to their owner's mood and the things around them; they care about their territory a lot.

Some people use them for waterfowl hunting because of their water repellant fur makes them ideal for it.

They are loveable dogs with families, and don't tend to be very aggressive. Labradors usually have yellow, black or brown furs.

Boxers

Boxers are a very lively, and playful breed, they are considered a puppy until they hit the age of three which gives them extra puppy years.

Boxers are great with children, because of their extended puppy years. They are very obedient, and do not require a lot of hard training, they listen very well.

It's best to train them at a young age. Boxers have ears that are pointed while tilted forward slightly, an obvious white underbelly, and at the tip of each foot there are some white parts.

The white parts can sometimes be on other parts of the body, but are most commonly on the shoulders and face.

Rottweiler

Rottweilers have been around a very long time, their lineage is traced back to ancient times where they were used as watchers for groups of cattle.

They are a very intelligent and strong breed of dogs. During wars, they are often used as military and police dogs. Rottweilers are also said to be fearless dogs, as well as very active, and they also love to play.

They are very good at learning things quickly, such as tricks, and rules. Rottweiler's are black and have tan spots on their legs, chest, face, cheeks, and sometimes under their tails.

They have triangles that are upside down on their chest, and each eyebrow has a unique spot.

Poodles

Poodles are a very loyal breed, and can be an excellent companion. Poodles are a calm breed of canines that have naturally very curly fur.

They are a variety of colors that Poodles come in, such as grey, white, black, blue, brown, and tan. Poodle training is usually more work than training of other breeds.

Poodles are mostly known for their lovely coats of curly fur, which require a lot of grooming to keep manageable, because you don't want their hair to tangle or clump up.

Dachshund

Dachshunds are also called wiener dogs because of their long torso/build. They have pointed faces, and short legs which are also another factor in their nickname.

They love to chase things, as well as hunt things, though they aren't as fast as other dogs. Dachshunds are very loyal and energetic, and they love to play. Despite appearing shy, there senses are very well-developed and astute.

Beagle

Beagles are often used for hunting because of their powerful sense of smell.

Training can be difficult because they are very strong willed which makes them obstinate. They are known to be very well tempered.

Beagles often look very gentle because of their large ears which are set low, their furs are often brown, black, white, or a mixture of both.

They often travel in packs, therefore being a pet dog might cause them some frustration or anxiety unless you plan on having more beagles as pets.

That was a simple overview of some popular breeds of canines. When choosing a dog for you, you need to think about certain factors such as its health, physical appearance, temperament, and which type of dog fits you best.

Also, you need to factor in your work, if you work a lot and will never be home then you need to find a dog that fits that type of living, or consider if you can handle having a dog at all.

Keep in mind that dogs need to be given positive and proper attention, love, and care.

Finding the Right Breeder

Canines are often said to be man's best friend, deciding to own a dog, no matter what size, takes a lot of responsibility.

There are certain things you have to do such as feeding it, grooming, making sure it's healthy, and doesn't get overweight, cleaning up after it, cleaning it, and making sure that you give it lots of love.

There are quite a few places that you can get a dog such as the pet store, a breeder, or the kennel. Don't always just disregard the kennel, they do have great dogs there, they are just dogs that have been abandoned and need lots of love.

If you want a purebred dog though, you need to find a breeder who has a good reputation to get the results you want.

Now, the right type of breeder and the breed of the dog you want go hand in hand. Breeders that are professional don't breed that often, and usually only do when a pair of purebreds are found that are healthy and temperament that will ensure the birth of healthy puppies.

Breeders also must have enough homes for the amount of offspring that will be birthed before they breed, and they usually have to be evaluated and appropriate.

Now if you know what type of breeder you need, then you should do some research by asking people that have used breeders, and talking to a number of breeders as feasible before make deciding who you are going to have breed the dog you want.

There are a lot of types of breeders in the world, and if you know which is the best, and understand that things can go wrong; if you can understand that then it will greatly influence the type of puppy that will be produced.

Truly, the ideal breeder would have the pair of canines tested for every type of disease and have all the information that has to do with the pair's lineage and family's health records on file. Even if the breeder mentions no issue in the history of the two dogs, you still need to ask just to be sure.

This shows the breeder that you truly have an interest in the parents of your future puppy, and that you want the best for it.

If you wish, you can also ask people who have also been given puppies of the pair to see if there were any problems. If you want a dog, then you need to have a fenced in, or secure yard and attend classes so that you are familiar with some of the problems and challenges you might face as a new puppy owner.

Breeders that have a good reputation and know what they are doing will have requirements that you have to meet before passing as a feasible dog owner.

These requirements are usually stated in the written contracts as with a requirement having to do with spaying or neutering which lowers the amount of registration of the puppies. This is all done so that there isn't an overpopulation issue, and for the protection of you, the owner.

The requirements that the breeder needs are not meant to delay producing, and giving you a dog, but to ensure that you are aware of what can and will happen as a dog owner and the responsibilities that go with it as well as make sure that the offspring will be going to a good home.

This is the thing that separates the breeders into two types; the ones that actually care about the health and well being of the dogs, and the breeders that are just in it to earn money. The first type is the breeder that you want.

Some of the most important factors in selecting a good breeder besides the food, and health attention given are the state of the father after the birth of the offspring and how well the puppies are cared for.

To check on the puppies and how they are being treated after birth, you should choose a breeder that is close by so that you can go see how the puppies are doing once in a while, and make sure that there aren't any problems.

Is Your Dog a Commonly Known Aggressive Breed?

Knowing whether or not your dog is an aggressive breed is very important thing to know before you decide on what kind of dog you want, that being said, a lot of people hear things that aren't true and don't know the truth about which dog breeds are most aggressive and which one's really aren't.

No dog is a bad breed, as some might say; they just have a bad connotation. Every dog has the ability to be trained, and that includes every breed.

One thing you need to know that as long as you have the right training for the breed and making sure they are familiar with other dogs and people.

Confidence is something that many people think that animals don't have the ability to have or not have, but that's not true.

As long as they have confidence it will help prevent aggressive behavior because they will be more secure with their dominance and self.

One of the main reasons dog's become so aggressive is because owners misconstrue what we thing they need, and how they are acting, or we don't even train them at all.

Some people might not believe that small dogs can be aggressive, but if you walk into the home of a small dog, you will sometimes see the complete opposite.

They sometimes display behavior of the aggressive nature such as snarling, growling, lunging, and biting, but people just ignore these behaviors because of the smallness of the dogs.

People should be aware of the fact that they can be dangerous, and even though they are small they can hurt people, especially the elderly and children.

This is usually because most people don't feel it is necessary to train small dogs.

The truth is any dog can be provoked to bite someone, regardless of breed. All owners of dogs should have their pets trained, and taught to follow needed commands such as sit, stay, lie, and come.

Taking dogs to an obedience class or a type of training is a way of preventing a lot of biting accidents, because of the simple fact that a trained dog is a calmer and more behaved dog.

Let's look at some various dog breeds that are known to be potentially aggressive:

- Lhasa Apso's can be snappish if they are irritated or surprised.

- Chow Chows try to assert their dominance by dominating other dogs, but are usually great with kids.

- Rottweiler's are usually pretty mellow, but are by nature protective of their owners. Strict training and socializing them with other dogs and humans is required to prevent aggression towards other dogs, and people he or she isn't familiar with. Regrettably, because of their protective instinct and size, they are usually trained wrong which promotes aggression.

- Chihuahuas are very wary of strangers, but loyal to the people who own them. They aren't tolerant of kids that handle them roughly, and will usually snap.

- Giant Schnauzers need an experienced owner because they are a very dominant type of dog. Therefore, without proper training they usually try and dominate other canines, and are liable to biting kids.

- Toy Poodles might snap if they are teased or startled, and can be cautious of strangers.

- Dachshunds are fast to bite and can be obstinate, envious, and testy.

- Pekinese are intolerant of rough kids, and are liable to jealousy.

• Mastiffs are usually good, and calm dogs, but they do need to be socialized with other canines and people, and they need to be trained to prevent an aggressive behavior towards other canines.

• German Shepherds need strict training, and a lot of socialization to prevent over protectiveness. They are also natural guard dogs; they don't like being left by themselves for long periods of time usually because they are people dogs.

• Bull Terriers are normally obedient, and calm. This breed does need to socialize with other dogs and people, as well as training to prevent an aggressive behavior towards other canines. One of the most important things to owning a Bull Terrier is that no matter how old they are, you need to make sure you give them attention and care.

Make sure that you recognize potential signs of dog aggression problems because it will make it easier to deal with these issues at an earlier stage. If you have any questions or doubts about anything having to do with dogs, then you should talk to a qualified veterinarian.

• American Pit Bulls are one breed that has a bad connotation, or reputation. The truth is any natural aggressive behavior in American Pit Bulls is usually towards other canines, and not humans.

American Pit Bulls are very much a people type of breed, but you still need to socialize them with other dogs a lot to help prevent an aggressive behavior towards other dogs. They are surprisingly tolerant of children.

Regrettably, bad training, and mistreatment by irresponsible people encourages aggression which is what attributes to their horrible reputation. Pit Bulls who have an aggressive behavior have a history of being abused or left behind.

Normal Problems That Dogs Have Concerning Aggression

Problems with behavior are a common thing in canines. If you look back at the history, and lineage of dogs, their relatives being coyotes, wolves, and various other animals of pure aggression puts them in the middle of a difficult situation.

While their brains are set to hunt, to travel in packs, and survive on their own we teach them the opposite.

Canines will usually show a variety of behavioral issues which have the possibility of getting out of control if the canines aren't trained properly.

Canines that already show signs of behavioral issues are headed towards bad things and worse behaviors if the owners permit it.

Canines are always able to learn how far they can go when they are presented with a challenge and will often get into bad situations if they are permitted to do what they want.

When you decide to handle your dog's behavioral issues, you need to understand the multiple, different causes of them. Every issue can be grouped with others and canines will continue to do them and they will evolve into worse things later if not restrained, and trained.

Signs to Recognize

Dogs with aggression express it in a couple of different types of behaviors including the most common, which are biting and barking.

An aggressive behavior is natural of animals of the pack variety, and is used to determine the ranking of the pack, as well as to be used as self-defense in times of danger.

Aggression has various levels and the amount of aggression the canine shows is determined by the amount of threat it feels from the person, animal, or situation.

Low Level Aggressive Behaviors

Some low level aggressive behaviors:

- Staring

- Aggressive Stance

- Growling

- Pushing

- Jumping on animals, and people to intimidate

- Doesn't Follow Commands

- Nipping At Legs or Heels. (This is not always a behavior were they are trying to specifically hurt you, it is more to herd you somewhere, but they should be taught not to do this.)

Aggressive behaviors that are considered low levels are usually what you see displayed first, unless it is a particularly threatening situation for the dog.

This is usually observed when you see dogs meet each other and interact for the first time. They are very stiff, and keep their tails and heads up, while their ears are pointed. They try and make themselves appear as big as possible, by standing as tall as they can.

Most often, one of the dogs will back down, and no more aggression with occur because the ranking has been decided. The size of the dog usually doesn't matter in the ranking, unless the aggression level goes higher.

High Level Aggressive Behavior

If low levels of aggressive behavior are not having the effect on the target, then the dog's behavior may rise to aggression of higher levels which include:

- Biting

- Snarling

- Snapping

- Showing of Teeth

- Jumping Up and Barking Aggressively

Higher levels of aggression in dogs go beyond mere warning to physical contact with the target, and attempting to bite.

This demonstrates a serious situation, and the dog should be taken somewhere were it isn't around other people and animals until it can be retrained.

An owner needs to be able to control their dog's aggression, as aggression is a normal type of behavior for dogs. The new dog will need to be trained to understand that this type of behavior is not appropriate.

As long as you socialize them with other humans and dogs early, and theirs a strict understanding of the relationship between you and your dog, you dog will not show aggression.

Getting a dog neutered will control the hormonal side of aggression, but not all aggression issues are caused by hormones.

Neutering and Spaying doesn't necessarily guarantee that they will be calm, such as breeds that are bred to be watch dogs or animals that herd will need specific training as to not be non-aggressive. Some breeds aren't as tolerant with children as others, just like some dogs aren't as good with other dogs, or animals.

Always remember to think about if the dog's natural behaviors will fit with you, or/and your family.
.

The Reasoning Behind Your Dog's Aggression

Dogs will and can show aggression if put in the right type of circumstances. Aggressive behavior is a natural response for dogs.

Therefore, it is very important to know what circumstances and such that is likely to cause aggression in your dog.

It's also important to remember that what you see and what the dog sees as an aggressive act that was unprovoked are different, because to the dog it could have been perfectly logical.

The major reasons for aggression in dogs are talked about below.

Territory Aggression

This form of aggression is used by dogs when they are defending their thought territory. Their 'territory' is any area that they are familiar will or have marked with their scent.

Even though you may be okay with your dog protecting your property, the dog may see the whole block or neighborhood as his or her territory to control/protect.

Possession Aggression

Dogs have the tendency to guard members of their family, and possessions. A dog's family may include other family pets, people, or even their favorite items such as toys or food.

This is the type of aggression that's pointed towards people or animals that are unfamiliar that are coming close to the dog's family, or possessions.

Transferred Aggression

Transferred aggression often happens when the dog becomes too excited or upset, and it gets aggressive with another person or dog, instead of the actual item.

Such as if someone was teasing a dog and they couldn't get to it, they might turn their aggression towards someone or another dog they can get too.

Ranking Aggression

Dogs like to travel in packs, which is why they are called pack animals, and in order to establish the ranking within the family which includes the human and other animals in the family they feel that they need to show aggression to establish their high rank.

Once the rank has been established, the dog does not like to be challenged. Owners often let their dogs think they are the highest ranking member in the family without knowing it, and that can often lead to difficulties controlling the dog. Aggression problems can also arise between dogs in the same family if they are battling for the top rank.

Aggression Caused By Fear

Dogs are similar to humans in the way they respond to a situation that causes fear which causes a fight or flight reaction. If the dogs respond with aggression they often do so by snarling, growling, or even biting.

There are different reaction in dogs because of their training methods, genetic disposition, and past experience. Even if it is in a calm environment, the dog might see something scary if they have been treated badly in the past.

Even dogs that would like to run from the fight, but can't have to go to aggression so that they can protect themselves.

If dogs feel that they are threatened they will resort to aggressive behavior, they could also resort to aggression if they feel that their position in the family, or their territory or things are threatened.

We don't understand all the things that set dogs off to make them act this way, but this is because we are humans. Aggressive behavior needs to be controlled so that there isn't any possible danger to any other animals or humans.

Punishment is very rarely a good way to teach that aggressive behavior is bad, unlike positive rewards in training works very well and shows the dogs that they are appreciated, and so is their hard work.

Ways to Stop Aggression in Your Dog

Getting a dog is a very large responsibility, one which should be taken very seriously even if the dog seems like it won't take a lot of work.

A lot of people buy puppies because of how cute they are without thinking about how much time, effort, and training they have to put in to take good care of it.

Don't make that mistake. Know all the information about the puppy you are thinking about getting.

The main factors in preventing aggressive behavior in dogs:

- Socialization with Other Animals and Humans

- Ranking Order Training

- Obedience Training

From the first day you bring your puppy home you should start all types of training and aggressive behavior prevention.

Ranking Order Training

Dogs are basically pack type animals. This means that they have a natural instinct to establish a ranking within the pack, and therefore need to know their place in the family.

A lot of owners don't understand this, and sometimes don't even comprehend that it's there. Therefore, the owner often then teaches their dog that they are higher than the owner, themselves, which can cause some problems in controlling the puppy.

You might wonder how this happens. It happens by letting the dog onto the beds, and furniture, letting the dog walk through the door before the owner, and feeding them food from their plates.

While it doesn't mean a lot to the owner, the dog begins to take these little things as signs that he is the Alpha Dog of the family. Therefore, if this happens the dog will begin to be more territorial over his territory, and the family members.

If the dog views himself as the alpha dog of the family he might not listen to any order or command given by someone else is his family because he sees them as below him.

This also means that the dog is likely to be more aggressive toward people and animals he doesn't know, and the dog will be less obedient.

Therefore, making your dominance known is extremely important.

If the dog understands that he's not in charge, you are, he will be more likely to listen to you, and he won't be as territorial or too protective over your family.

Ways to Establish Your Dominance:

- Walk through doorways first, and make your dog wait.

- After you have eaten, then feed your dog.

- Don't let your dog(s) onto the beds or furniture.

- Don't let your dog have scraps from your plate.

- Train your dog in obedience.

Socialization with Other Animals and Humans

Exposing your dog to a lot of different and new situations is of high important. Which includes introducing them to a lot of others dogs and people.

They will be more confident the more situations they are exposed too, and will then be more likely to not display aggression due to fear, which happens to be a common consequence of a puppy not being exposed to other dogs and people.

It is also extremely important because it promotes tolerance of unfamiliar dogs or people, which lessens the likeliness of dominance and territorial aggression behavior showing up.

The first couple of months after you bring your puppy home are some of the most important because it's a good idea to take him with you to the places you go so that you can expose him to other dogs, people, and new situations.

Make sure your dog is fully vaccinated first so that your dog doesn't catch any infections.

Some helpful tips:

•	Your puppy should be introduced to your friends, family, and neighbors, so as he is familiar with them.

•	Take your new dog for walks and go to the dog park, so that he can greet other dogs and people that he is unfamiliar with.

•	Set up doggy play dates for your puppy with a person that you know and their dog.

•	Enforce good behavior by encouraging play that is friendly.

•	Take your puppy to classes for puppies, such as obedience classes and house training classes.

- Don't forget to always socialize your dog even after he is out of his puppy years.

Obedience Training

A lot of owners have the misconception that obedience training should wait, or isn't important until the puppy is at least six months or older.

The truth is that puppies can begin being taught and learning basic commands as earlier as when they are around eight weeks old.

Therefore, it is also recommended that training should begin as early as is possible so that there isn't time for your puppy to develop bad behaviors or habits which can in turn be difficult to stop.

It will be a lot easier to control your dog if you teach them to follow commands as soon as possible. Teaching them earlier isn't only to make it easier for you, but make it safer for them as well.

This type of training also enforces your Top Dog position in the family. Also, don't make the mistake of thinking that just because your dog is small you shouldn't teach him basic commands because small dogs can be just as aggressive as large dogs, and should be trained as so.

It's recommended that you should keep your lessons short while your dog is still learning, which means that you need to make them often. A dog will learn more in 5 five minute sessions over a day, rather than one twenty five minute lesson.

Another recommendation is that you should continue with lessons on obedience throughout the dog's whole life so that he doesn't forget what the commands mean.

If you feel that you can't teach your puppy the various basic commands, then think about trying obedience classes. Obedience classes are also good for socializing with other dogs.

Suggested Basic Commands to teach your dog:

- Stay

- Sit

- Drop It

- Come

- Off

You may have noticed that the three ways for preventing aggressive behavior and aggression cover some of the same thing.

This is why it is very important to use all three ways because you will find that each one helps reinforce the other ones.

These methods are not flawless; they will help a lot in preventing bad behaviors in your puppy, especially aggressive behavior. They have also been known to make a large difference in changing already existing aggressive behavior problems.

How to Control Redundant Barking

Barking that is redundant or excessive is a very common behavioral issue in canines. Besides the fact that it is a very annoying to hear, it is also stressful to the household, and the neighborhood.

Handling this issue can be done in a couple of ways. It's extremely important to train your puppy to not bark excessively as young as feasible. It's not impossible to teach an older dog to cease barking excessively, it is very difficult because they were not taught that it was bad while growing up.

Using Bark Control

There are a variety of different things that are used to control barking also know as bark control, though they may or may not curb barking of the excessive nature.

How much each device works for you depends on how your dog reacts to it, and whether or not it's enough of a reason for them to stop barking.

There are a couple of devices that come in a collar form that do various things. For example, some collars emit a loud ultrasonic sound when the dog barks so that they learn if they bark then they will hear that loud sound, and there are also electronic collars which let out a small shock to the dog when they bark. Electronic collars are not legal everywhere.

Barking: How to Punish It

Dogs seem to love to bark; therefore they try and bark at everything. You, as an owner, or soon to be owner need to know how to punish your dog in a human way that shows them that barking is a unnecessary behavior at most times.

Therefore, whenever redundant barking happens, an owner will need to be able to punish their dog in a way that demonstrates that it must be stopped immediately.

Here are some common ways used to punish dogs in a humane way:

- Spray Bottle Filled with Citronella Oil or Water - This type of oil has a strong scent which is why dogs generally dislike it. When you spray them with it while they are barking, they will associate their barking with the unpleasant spray, and smell and stop.

They will eventually get used to it if it is used too often. Therefore, it's a good idea to only use it occasionally and make sure you don't get it in their eyes, or any open wounds.

- Tapping the Nose - Of the dog's body parts, the nose is one of the most sensitive.

Tapping the dog's nose once lightly usually is enough to get them to stop their barking. If you do this each time redundant barking happens it will help the dog learn not to bark. Don't hit their nose harder than a light tap because it can actually hurt the dog, or even made the nose bleed.

• Quieting with Noise - Noise can be very useful in getting dogs to stop barking. For example, if you whistle loudly, snap your fingers loudly, or clap it will most likely stop them from barking, and over time will teach them not to bark redundantly.

You also need to remember that not every time your dog barks warrants a punishment, you need to decide whether or not the barking was okay for the situation or occurrence before punishing him.

Stopping Dog Aggression over Food

A possible dangerous behavior that happens when your dog becomes territorial over its food dish or any type of food that he believes is his is called food aggression.

This aggressive behavior can be presented by snapping, growling, or even trying to bite another human or dog that goes near their food.

As you know, any type of aggression in a dog is potentially dangerous and not appropriate. Therefore, this type of behavior should be stopped, and addressed so that your dog can be a happy member of your house.

If your dog starts showing signs of this type of aggression, you should immediately move your dog's feeding area. Also, if you have more than one dog in your house, then you should make sure they are not together during feeding time.

If your dog starts have food aggression then you should start feeding them on a schedule. If you're not sure of the right type of feeding schedule, contact your animal specialist or veterinarian.

Next, you need to assert yourself as the 'alpha' of your family, which includes the dogs. Your dog needs to understand that you are the one who gives the food and realize that you are above him in the ranking of your home. Once he realizes this, there will be less of a possibility of him displaying aggression towards you when you come near his food dish.

Now, the next step in this process is to start being there when your dog is eating. Then, for about one to two weeks you should start feeding your dog from your hands and other household members hands directly(not including children), and don't let him eat out of the food bowls.

Once you have done that for about two weeks, which during those two weeks you should be feeding the dog twice a day in this way, get the dog's food dish and put it on the floor.

Then, put handfuls of food into the bowl slowly. Such as, put a handful in, and wait for your dog to finish it then add some more.

Next, fill the food dish half full, and then add the rest with your hands.

After two more weeks, the final step is to fill the dish all the way and then teach the dog to wait and sit until your signal to start eating.

This last step should be used for the rest of the dog's life.

The Dog's Biting Problems - What You Can Do

There's no guaranteed way to make sure that your dog will never attack or bite anyone.

That being said, there are things you can do so that you can make it less likely to happen and reduce the risks.

Here are some things people do to deal with it.

Think about everything before taking in a puppy or dog and once you decide to take one in, choose carefully.

A lot of people who are irresponsible have bought/adopted a puppy because they thought they looked adorable, without thinking about the responsibility of owning a dog.

Because once the cute puppy grows up into a dog and needs a lot of food, grooming, exercise, and training, the owners freak out and either give the dog away or lock it up in the back yard.

There are two good sources of information having to do with pet behavior and match-ability which are; a veterinarian and tons of helpful websites on the internet that explain everything there is to know about various breeds.

- Teach the dog to obey basic commands such as come, sit, no, off, and stay. When you do the training activity, add some fun games to it.

- Consider getting your dog spayed or neutered, because the truth is that neutered dogs are less likely to bite or attack.

- Make sure that your dog is socialized well, and properly. Even if you are getting a puppy, make sure you socialize him with different people, situations, and animals so that he feels calm around them.

- Know your dog well, and watch for signs of aggressive or fearful behavior, sickness, or discomfort.

- If you want to decrease the likelihood of your kids being bitten by your dog then wait until they are old enough (seven or eight) before getting one. This way the kids can help with the dog and are old enough to be able to treat the dog nicely.

- Make sure you get the dog vaccinated.

Dogs deserve to be respected, just like humans. You should always make them feel like a true member of the family.

If your dog spends a lot of time outside in the yard alone, or chained up he could possible become a highly dangerous animal.

Unlike, the dogs that are loved, watched over, and socialized well by their owners rarely bite.

If you want your dog to connect with you and other dogs then you need to spend time with your dog and give it some tender loving care.

Signs

This type of behavior (aggression) doesn't just happen after one day.

There is a path that leads up to it, and if you pay attention, you can spot it and stop it before it reaches the end of the path.

Dogs get to the aggressive stage a lot more quickly than other dogs, but they all follow a similar path to aggressive behavior.

Knowing what some early warning signs are is very important because the earlier you catch it developing, the easier it can be to fix it.

Some warning signs of pre-aggression are listed below.

If you find your dog doing anything of this list, then you need to stand straight and let him know that you are the leader of the family.

- Starts guarding food, toys, and furniture. Snaps, growls, or tenses when you come near it.

- Makes you give him attention by pawing, whining, or nudging you. This is the dog demonstrating bossiness.

- Sits and stares at you, paces by your feet, or nudges you for food while you eat.

- Starts to ignore you and your commands, even if he knows the commands. He is showing disobedience.

Why are these signs dangerous?

Disobedience itself isn't particularly dangerous though it can be, and getting your attention and eating some of your food won't hurt you physically.

Therefore, it's very important to notice these signs, and stop, his behaviors because they show that your dog is starting to think he is a higher rank than you in the family.

You want to know the absolute sign that your dog accepts that you are higher ranking over him? Obedience.

So when he begins to test you with those behaviors listed above, he is questioning your authority over him.

This is a definite warning sign that he isn't respecting you as much as he should be in order to understand who's in charge and so that you and your dog can live together safely, and happily.

Finally, this means that you need to stop this behavior before it gets any farther, and develops into something much worse.

What to Do If Your Dog Displays Early Warning Signs

First thing, you need to understand the idea of the alpha dog of the family, or the top ranking person in the family.

In short, it relates to who is seen to be in charge of the family.

The alpha is the lead dog of the pack. Alphas have a certain type of behaviors that only they are allowed to do, dogs of lesser rank in the pack are never allowed to act like alphas.

Usually, if a lesser rank does in fact try to do so, the alpha will defend his alpha position with a show of aggression.

Dogs are described as pack animals, which means that they feel the most calm and safe when they feel someone is in charge, even if it isn't them.

Therefore, if nobody in your house is taking the alpha position in ways that the dog recognizes then he will try and fill that spot himself.

Here are some ways for you to assert your authority so that your dog understands:

One of the most important things to remember is to not include any human motives or values on this dog alpha-related behavior; wolf/dog packs have alphas because it ensures that the pack will survive. Don't think that just because your dog is trying to take the role as alpha in the house that it's because he wants too.

It's because his brain tells him that someone has to be the alpha in the house in order to survive, and since to him it seems that no one else is stepping up to do that, he feels that he has too.

Aggressive behavior comes into the equation when you challenge your dog's authority as the leader or alpha of the family.

Such as if you tried to push him off of the couch, or you take his food from him.

Also, making him do something that he doesn't want to do would be seen as a challenge. Most of the time you don't even realize that you are challenging his authority, it just seems normal to you.

It doesn't matter if you think he's the alpha in the situation or not. It's that fact that he thinks he is, and it's how he sees himself as the alpha in correlation with you being a lower ranking than him that's controlling how he acts.

It's completely natural for him to use aggression to protect himself and his position if he has been allowed to believe that he is alpha dog.

Just the fact that your dog sees himself as alpha means that eventually someone will challenge his authority whether they mean to or not.

As seeing himself as an alpha dog, he will not take the fact that he has been challenged kindly, and this is where the dominant-aggressive behavior starts.

The understanding and concept of alpha behavior, is relatively complex and difficult.

There are a lot of different ways that you can prove to your dog that you are the alpha in the household and he is the lesser ranking member, not the other way around.

The same way that there is a lot of ways that tons of dogs all over the world show alpha dominance over their owners, without the owners even realizing it.

Therefore, you need to make sure that your dog clearly understands that you are in charge and are the alpha in the family.

Although, occasionally dogs are able to go on through the early stages of the behavior talked about above without anyone noticing the signs or stopping them from doing it.

You can recognize when your dog has progressed to the late stages because he will stop putting up with your corrections of his dominance or disobedience, and will respond with some powerful warning signals.

Also, know the difference between aggression, and the threat of aggression.

The threat is your canine's way of telling you and warning you to step off before he escalates to aggression.

Some classic warning signals of pre-aggressive behavior in the late stages:

• Biting or a Bite that doesn't leave the skin broken

• Barking or Growling with Teeth Bared

• Snarling, or Deep Growling

• Loud barking while standing straight and big, leaning towards you with ears erect, rigid posture, and tail twitching slowly.

What To Do If Your Dog Displays Any Of These Signs:

This type of behavior is basically the final thing that he will show before he attacks someone.

Therefore, a dog acting like this towards his owners has some serious problems with dominance which need to be addressed and dealt with by someone who is experienced.

If at any point you feel threatened by how your dog is acting then you may want to think about contacting a professional dog trainer or veterinarian who has dealt with aggressive dogs in the past.

Don't be afraid to ask for help.

When You Should Hire Professional Help:

- You are scared.

- Your dog guards toys, food, furniture, or anything else with enough ferocity that you can't go near it.

- Your dog bites you and it breaks the skin.

Why You Should Hire Professional Help

There are two main reasons why:

Trying to handle a difficult and frightening problem by yourself without someone else with experience could put you at risk.

If you react to your dog somehow in the wrong way, he might try and bite you.

Help from someone inexperienced could hurt the dog's development and not be good for it. If you mess up or are too frightened by the dog's behavior to continue to do something, then you could end up encouraging the exact behavior that you are trying to stop.

We are also not trying to say that you should just give up and call the nearest dog specialist right away.

Quite the opposite in fact, a large percentage of dogs listen and learn a lot from the training techniques said in this chapter. We are only saying that if you feel like you can't handle the situation then you shouldn't be afraid or embarrassed to go looking for help.

Things You Should and Shouldn't Do Concerning Dog Aggression

Should Do:

•	Take care, if you have the suspicion that your dog might act with aggression towards other animals or people then watch him closely and have him wear a leash or muzzle if necessary.

•	Make regular checkups for your dog at the vet's office to make sure that he or she is healthy and happy. Pain can be a big factor in turning a calm dog into an aggressive one.

•	Spay or neuter your dog. It's an effective way to reduce the random aggression in dogs of either sex by a lot.

•	Put your dog in time out. It might sound silly, but it works. When dogs get too excited they act in ways that they normally wouldn't. So put him in timeout in his crate/kennel, away from the action so that he can cool down. Leave him there for about five to ten minutes. Don't keep him in there too long or it will defeat the purpose.

•	Make sure that you socialize your dog from a very young age and throughout his whole life, it is very important because it teaches them how to talk to other dogs and how to act around other humans. The most important time for socialization is between the ages of sixteen weeks and ten weeks, but if your dog is already older than this, don't worry just start socializing as soon as possible. Don't forget to use a leash in public.

Should Not:

•   Play-fighting. If your dog has ever shown signs of aggression or aggressive behavior in the past, then this will just increase the tendency for aggression to show up. It's okay if you don't do it often, and your dog knows the limits of playing.

•   Use food to bribe your dog. Treats that are food are definitely useful, but not when it has to do with dealing with aggression. When you are training your dog to be anti-aggressive, your dog's respect for you plays a very big part. A bribe with food for behavior that is good doesn't endanger his respect for you.

•   Abuse, humiliate, or punish your dog. If you think that punishing your dog during anti-aggression training is production, then you are extremely wrong. It will just deteriorate any loyalty and trust your dog has for you. This makes future training harder.

Once you've applied all or any of these helpful hints that apply to your situation and dog, give it some time and don't expect it to happen overnight. New habits can take awhile to form.

If after a couple of weeks your dog is still acting wrong, then it's time to do something further.

The main components of a training program for aggression having to do with dominance are:

- Positively rewarding behavior that is submissive.

- Improved overall obedience.

- Showing them the right thing to do about aggressive behavior without causing more aggression.

Common Dog Aggression Training Guidelines

Things to remember:

•	Wait until your dog gives you something first, before giving him something. This shows that you are the boss.

•	Don't reward any behavior that isn't positive. If your dog is acting badly, don't yell at him; don't give him any attention at all because the attention is the reward for your dog. Ignore him completely until he starts acting better.

•	Pet, talk to, and praise your dog whenever you witness him acting good, because it makes him aware of the fact that he can earn your attention and affection in a positive way. Therefore, as time continues he'll begin to group your reactions with his doings, and do something good instead of just stopping the bad behavior.

•	No games that can lead to something aggressive, So even when you are just playing tug of war, rough-housing, or tag, be careful so that it doesn't escalate to something of the aggressive nature.

•	Only let him chew on one toy or thing per day, if you let him have any more, then he starts thinking of it as his. Don't leave the toys lying around, hand the toy to him after he does something good in the morning and then at the end of the day, put it away.

If your dog has a problem with guarding and likes to guard his toys then don't let him have any until the obedience sets in.

•	Don't hit or yell at your dog. It doesn't help.

•	Think smart, don't let him off of his leash in publish, and keep the amount of leash between you and him short.

•	Have your dog exercise as much as possible, and take him for a long walk at least once a day. Dogs that aren't exercised enough are tense, jumpy, and more likely to be aggressive. Remember, don't let him off the leash, it's a privileged that must be earned.

Dog Fighting, What To Do About It

Fighting among dogs happens for a variety of reasons.

Trust is always a problem because new dogs coming into a territory may want to take over it or get too close.

Dogs which aren't used to being around other dogs will usually cause a fight because of the fact that the new dogs are strangers and intruding on their area, and trying to claim it for themselves.

Stopping fighting in your dog is encouraged but if you are going to do so you need to be careful. Often, dogs won't listen to anyone else during a fight, and will be aggressive with anyone who tries to get in the middle of the fight.

Spraying the dogs with the hose or a very loud noise can help to stop the fighting and aggression. If a dog that doesn't live in your house comes into your yard and starts a fight with your dog, it is important to remove the dog from your yard.

This type of aggression is caused by dogs fighting over territory.

What to Do In a Dog Fight

Don't freak out if your dog gets into a fight with another dog, it's very important to stay calm and not get in the middle of it.

This is obvious common sense because your skin isn't going to stand a chance against two dogs with canine teeth.

Though it's easy to forget that when you are watching your dog fight another dog.

Some owners with not a lot of common sense sometimes make the mistake of trying to separate the dogs by reaching into the middle of the fight to do so.

This is obviously a bad idea because in a dog fight the dog's adrenaline is very high and your dog is not thinking clearly.

The truth is that there is a risk of you being bitten by either of the dogs which includes your own.

Fights sometimes end quickly because one dog gives up, and accepts defeat. During other times though, especially if the dogs are matched in size and strength then it can turn into a long fight.

That's when it becomes crucial to take action.

Conclusion

In conclusion, getting a dog comes with a lot of responsibility and thought beforehand, and then a lot of hard work, and loving care once you actually get the puppy.

All dogs can be aggressive, but there are also a lot of ways to stop them from being aggressive and having problems.

Think about it.

If you find this book helpful and you love it, please tell your friends. Thank you.

Printed in Great Britain
by Amazon.co.uk, Ltd.,
Marston Gate.